JONAH

Jonah was a prophet who lived in Old Testament times. A prophet spoke out and told people what God wanted them to know. Jonah was known as the son of Amittai and he came from a place called Gath Hepher.

God gave him a message to take to the people who lived in Nineveh. Nineveh was a big city and the people who lived in it were very bad. God was not pleased with them and wanted Jonah to go and tell the people that he was angry with them.

However, Jonah did not want to do this and so he ran away. He headed for a place called Joppa, which was a port. Many boats sailed from Joppa and Jonah found one that was going to a place called Tarshish. He paid his fare and got on board. He hoped to run away from God and the job which God wanted him to do.

However, no-one can run away from God, as Jonah was about to find out ...

The story of Jonah can be found in the book of Jonah Chapters 1–4

MAZE

Here we see Jonah running to Joppa. Which ship will he get on board?

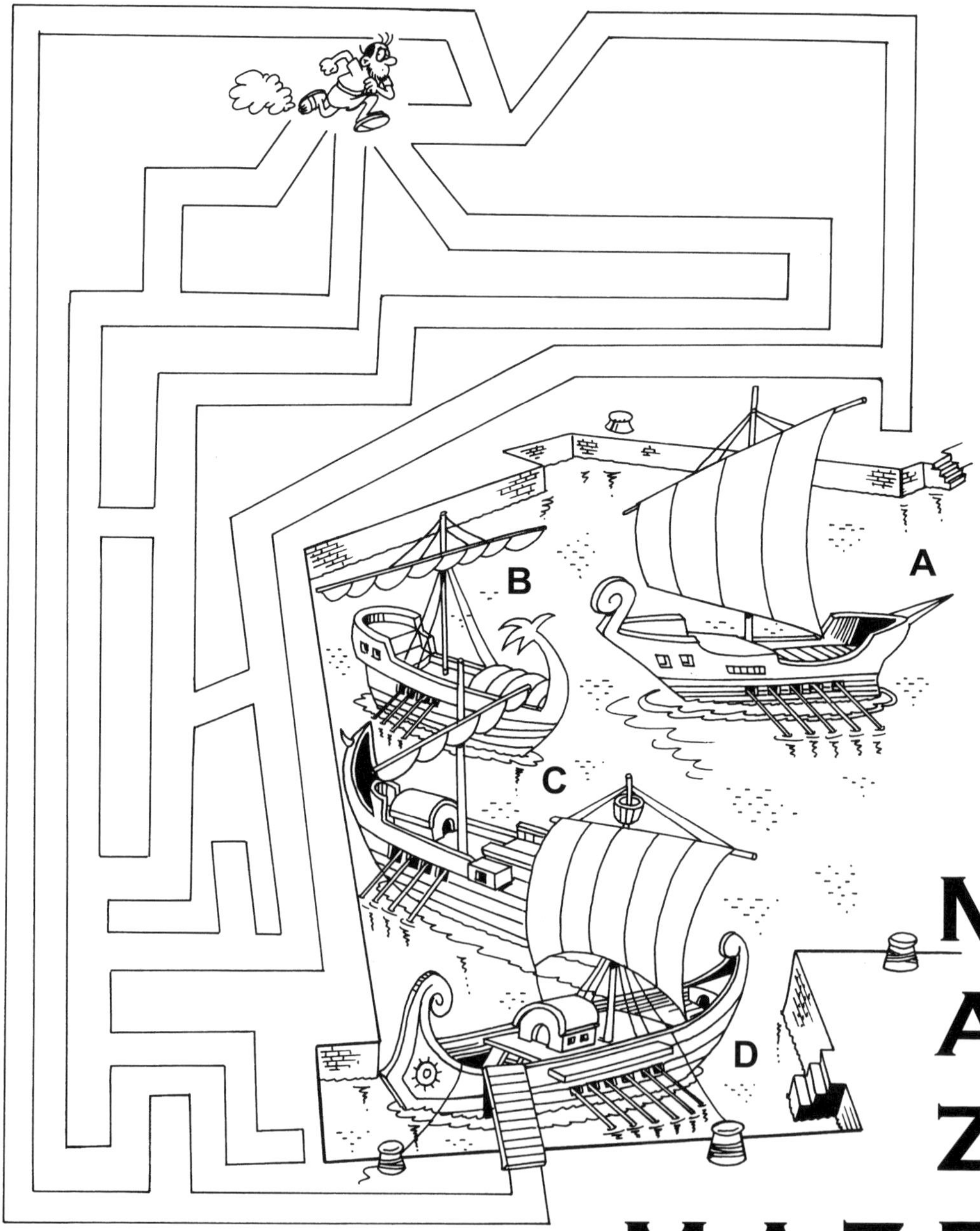

MAZE

A storm began ...

but Jonah had gone below deck and had settled down to sleep. He wasn't aware of all the problems that were going on around him. Eventually, the captain of the ship came to him and woke him up.

What do you think the captain said? Put your answer in the speech bubbles and then check the answers at the end of the book to find out what he actually said to Jonah.

Colour in the parts of the picture which have a dot, to find out how the rest of the sailors felt.

SPOT THE DOT & COLOUR IN

Unjumble & join

God sent a very strong wind and a fierce storm. There was a danger that the boat would not survive the storm ... it might break up and sink ... everything and everyone could be lost!

Can you match the pairs and unjumble the stormy words?

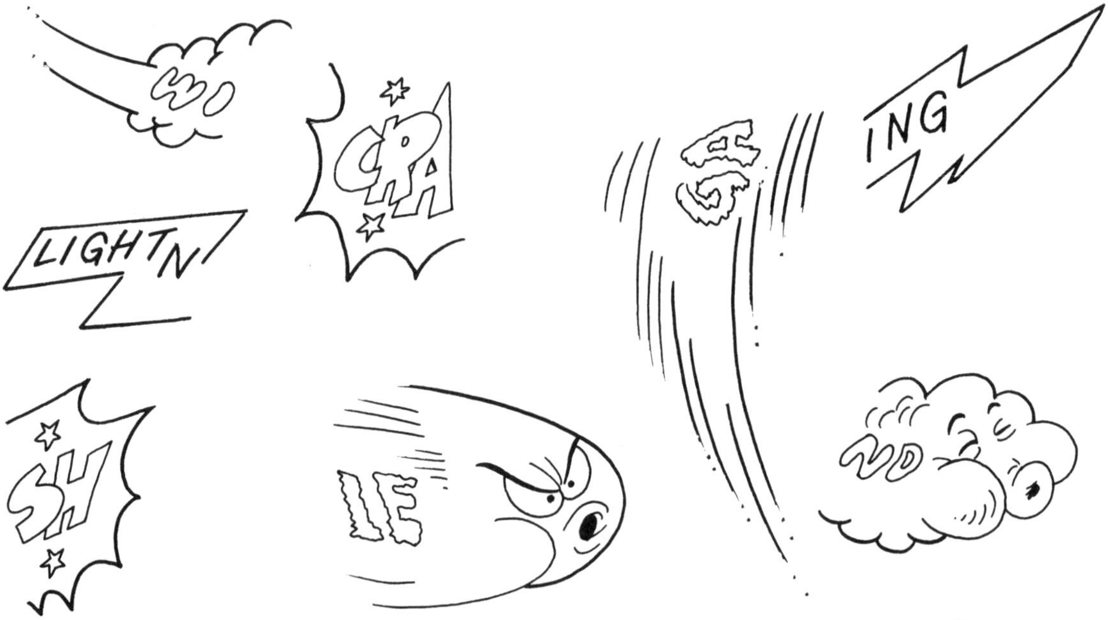

As the storm raged the sailors got more and more worried. They decided to try and find out for themselves why this dreadful storm had hit them. They cast lots and found that Jonah was to blame. They asked Jonah to tell them about himself ...

Can you complete the fact file on Jonah?

FACT FILE

Name: ....

Father's name: ....

Home town: ....

Occupation: ....

Religion: ....

Reason for travelling:

....

....

....

Portrait of Jonah

Finger print

Personal photograph

Finger print

Imagine you have to tell the sailors about yourself ...

FACT FILE

Name: ....

Surname: ....

Home town: ....

Description: *(e.g. hair colour)*

....

Religion: ....

Things I enjoy:

....

....

....

As the sailors found out about Jonah they became more and more worried. They wanted to know what they should do to make the sea calm again.

What did Jonah tell them to do?

The men didn't listen to what Jonah said. Instead they tried to row the boat back to the shore, but the sea was too wild for them. In the end they had to throw Jonah into the raging sea.

Immediately the sea calmed down. When the sailors saw this they began to fear God.

WHERE'S JONAH?

God created a huge variety of wonderful creatures which live under the sea.

How many can you name? Can you find Jonah hidden in the water?

I can see ...

Jonah found himself in the sea, but even this was part of God's plan for him. A huge fish was ready to swallow him up.

Which fish will swallow him up?

Jonah was in the fish for three days and three nights.
Can you find the numbers hidden in these sentences?

a) We need to get wood to mend the whole.

b) We have a sail on each mast.

c) The ferry boat went yesterday.

d) Look at all the stuff I've packed.

e) The cargo ship was called a freighter.

WORDSEARCH

Can you find the following words from the story?

MESSAGE **JOPPA** **JONAH** **FISH**
THROW **STORM** **THREE** **AFRAID**

X	C	E	E	G	A	S	S	E	M
C	C	A	P	T	A	I	N	O	S
J	O	N	T	H	R	E	E	S	W
S	A	I	L	O	R	S	S	T	A
T	S	E	S	J	O	N	A	H	L
R	L	O	N	P	S	W	H	V	L
J	E	W	I	X	Y	H	S	Z	O
O	E	O	N	T	P	I	I	O	W
P	P	R	E	J	O	P	F	P	A
P	S	H	V	D	I	A	R	F	A
A	W	T	E	M	R	O	T	S	Y
T	H	K	H	A	V	E	N	I	O

SWALLOW **SAILORS** **NINEVEH** **SHIP**
ASLEEP **CAPTAIN**

WORDSEARCH

God heard Jonah's prayer

While Jonah was inside the fish he prayed to God. Can you make sense of his prayers?

What happened next...?

JOIN THE DOTS

God heard Jonah's prayer and made the fish spit Jonah out onto dry land. **Where did Jonah land? Join the dots to find out.**

Can you help the fisherman make sense of his catch? Cross out all the q's and b's in the message to find out what God asked Jonah to do next.

SPOT THE DIFFERENCE

Can you find eight differences between the pictures?

SPOT THE DIFFERENCE

WORD PUZZLE

CLUES - ACROSS

3. The sailor's threw Jonah .... the sea. (4)
6. The ship was caught in this. (5)
8. The man who ran. (5)
12. Life was not this for Jonah. (4)
14. Sailors use this to tie things down. (4)
15. Something Jonah needed to do. (4)
16. God sent the fish to .... Jonah. (6)

CLUES - DOWN

1. This was how the sea was. (5)
2. What swallowed Jonah? (4)
4. Jonah went ...... the side of the ship. (4)
5. Where Jonah ran to. (5)
7. Jonah might have found this useful to help him find his way. (3)
9. Where Jonah should have gone. (7)
10. Jonah might have shouted this. (4)
11. The number of nights Jonah was in the fish. (5)
13. Another name for ocean. (3)
17. Eventually the fish gave Jonah ... (2)

Which way now?

At last Jonah decided to obey God and he set off for Nineveh. It was a huge city, and would take him about three days to walk across it.

Which path will take him to Nineveh?

Jonah walked through the city for one day and then he stopped and began to preach to the people.

Can you crack the code to find out what he said?

1.6.20.5.18 6.15.18.20.25

____

4.1.25.19 14.9.14.5.22.5.8

____

23.9.12.12 2.5 4.5.19.20.18.15.25.5.4

____

A	B	C	D	E	F	G	H	I	J	K	L	M	N	O
1	2	3	4	5	6	7	8	9	10	11	12	13	14	15

P	Q	R	S	T	U	V	W	X	Y	Z
16	17	18	19	20	21	22	23	24	25	26

When the king heard what Jonah was saying he became very upset. He tore his clothes, put on sackcloth and sent a message throughout the whole land.

Find the missing words hidden in the picture and use them to complete the message to find out what the king said. One word is used twice in the text and picture.

When God saw that the people had changed their ways, he decided not to punish them.

WORDSEARCH

A	D	E	S	T	R	O	Y	A	S	R
E	N	R	O	F	J	H	O	H	V	H
T	I	G	O	O	M	S	N	T	G	P
H	N	A	P	R	E	A	C	H	C	N
T	E	R	A	T	S	F	A	H	I	O
O	C	I	T	Y	S	N	N	S	G	K
L	R	I	N	K	B	G	G	I	N	N
C	J	O	N	I	N	R	R	N	I	P
K	T	P	U	N	I	I	Y	U	K	Y
C	A	N	N	G	E	E	R	P	L	L
A	E	G	A	S	S	E	M	D	A	A
S	F	D	E	C	L	A	R	E	W	W

How quickly can you find the following?

destroy	king	forty	ash	preach
eat	drink	punish	sackcloth	message
city	angry	walking	declare	

Jonah saw and heard all that was happening around him. He hadn't expected things to turn out like this. How did Jonah really feel about the people's behaviour and God's decision?

 _ _ _ _ _ was very  _ _ _ _ _ _ _ _

and became  _ _ _ _ _ _ . He

knew that God was  _ _ _ _ _ _ _ and

kind, and that he would change his  _ _ _ _ _ .

 _ _ _ _ _ asked God to let him  d _ _ .

God spoke to Jonah and asked him if he thought it was right for him to be angry. Jonah thought about this ...

Colour the picture

Jonah left the city by the road to the east. He made himself a shelter, sat down and waited to see if anything would happen to the city. While he was sitting there, God made a plant grow up over him to protect him from the hot sunshine. This plant helped Jonah to feel happier.

Sadly, early the next morning, God made a worm come along to destroy the plant. The plant withered and died and Jonah no longer had shelter from the blazing sun. Even worse, God made a burning east wind come along - this made Jonah feel so faint that he wanted to die.

Can you find ten differences in these two pictures?

SPOT THE DIFFERENCE

SPOT THE DIFFERENCE

What would you say?

God wanted Jonah to understand that he cared very much for the people of Nineveh and was prepared to forgive them.

If you had been a journalist in Bible times how would you have written Jonah's story for your newspaper?

Nineveh News

MAN ALIVE AFTER THREE DAYS IN FISH!

The man who ran

For this game you will need a dice and counters for the number of players. Follow the trail and get to Nineveh as fast as you can.

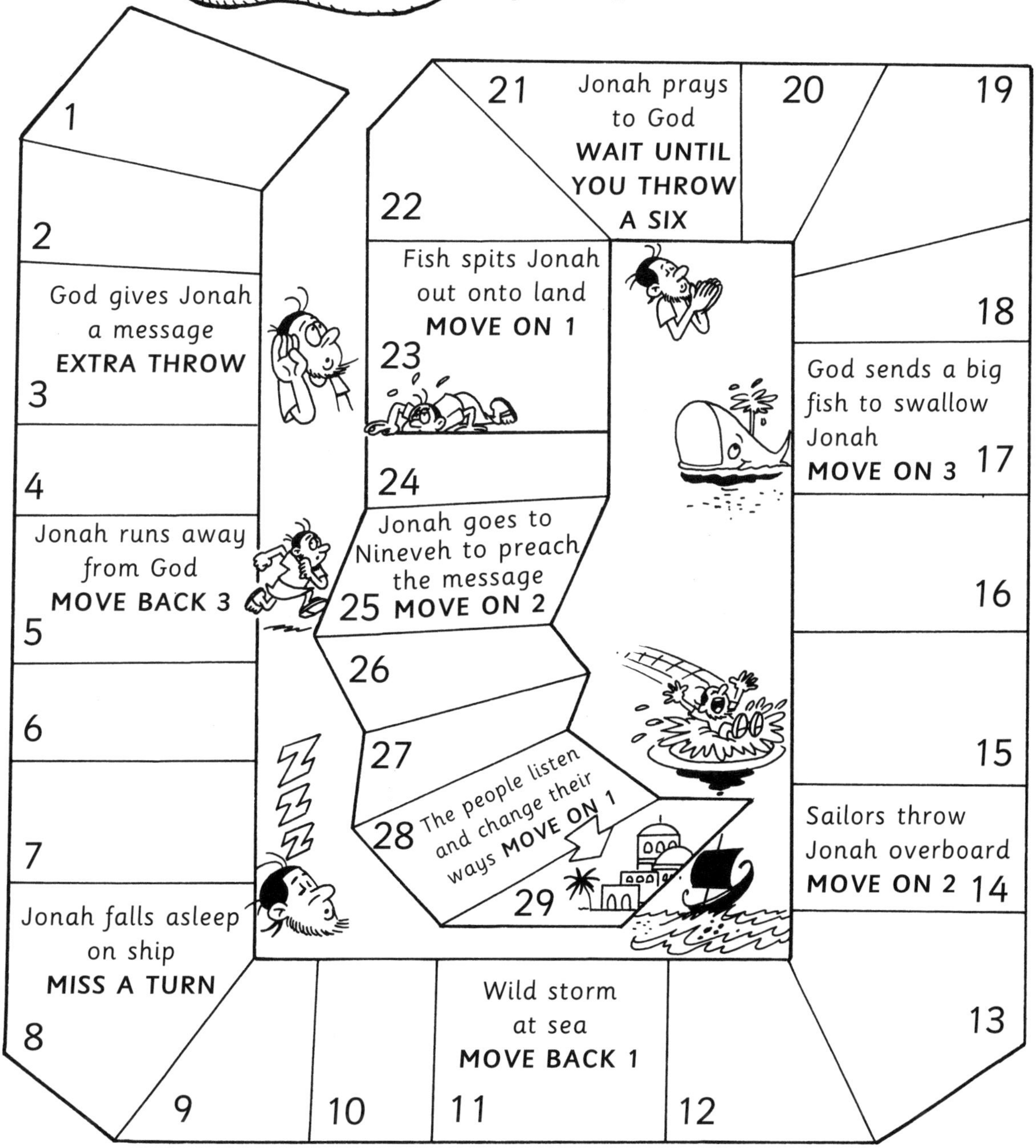

Can you remember ?

How much can you remember about the man who ran? Test your memory with this short quiz. Give yourself one point for every correct answer and colour in your score on the chart.

POINTS

1. **Where did Jonah come from?**
   a) Nineveh   b) Tarshish   c) Gath Hepher   ______

2. **Where did God tell him to go to?**
   a) Joppa   b) Nineveh   c) Amitti   ______

3. **What did Jonah do?**
   a) went to Nineveh   b) stayed where he was
   c) ran away to Joppa   ______

4. **When Jonah was on the boat what was the weather like?**
   a) stormy   b) fair   c) snow showers   ______

5. **What did the sailors do to Jonah?**
   a) gave him some food   b) gave him a shave
   c) threw him overboard   ______

6. **Who took care of Jonah?**
   a) his family   b) the people of Nineveh   c) God   ______

7. **How long was Jonah in the fish?**
   a) three days and nights   b) a week   c) two days   ______

8. **What did Jonah do while he was in the fish?**
   a) slept   b) prayed   c) read a book   ______

9. **How did Jonah get back to land?**
   a) he swam ashore   b) he used a boat
   c) the fish spat him onto the land   ______

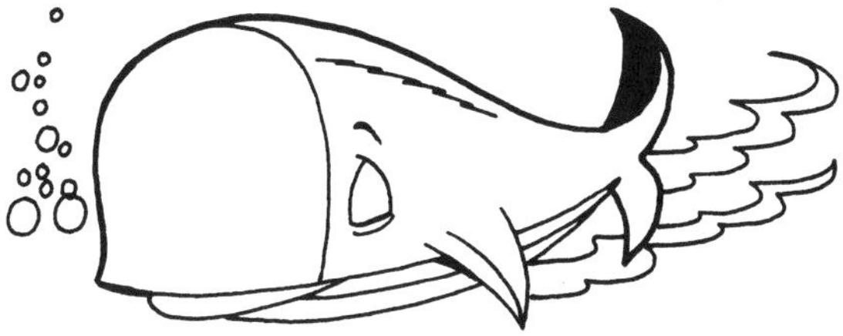

Can you remember?

10. Where did Jonah go next? POINTS

a) Nineveh b) back to Joppa

c) the local fishing club ______

11. What did he do there?

a) bought some food b) started preaching

c) did some shopping ______

12. Did people listen to him?

a) No b) Yes c) some did ______

13. What did God do?

a) he destroyed them b) he forgave them

c) he ignored them ______

14. How did Jonah feel about the situation?

a) he was angry b) he was happy

c) he didn't care ______

How did you score?

Colour in the number of fish which match your score e.g. if you scored 10 points, colour 10 fish.

Answers

Page 2:	D
Page 3:	'Why are you sleeping? Get up and pray!' Scared.
Page 4:	Wind, crash, gale, lightning.
Page 5:	Jonah, Amittai, Gath Hepher, prophet, Jewish, running away from what God had asked him to do.
Page 6:	Throw me overboard and the sea will calm down. This is all my fault.
Page 8:	4. (a) two, (b) one, (c) twenty, (d) five, (e) eight.
Page 10:	(1) I went down to the depths of the sea. (2) While I was in distress I called to God. (3) God heard me and answered me. (4) I thought I was lost forever. (5) God saved me from death.
Page 11:	God told Jonah to pick himself up and head to Nineveh and there tell the people the message from God.
Page 12:	Camel's eye, man's head covering, Jonah's belt, Jonah's sandal, stone missing near city, window shadow, worm sleeping, leaf missing.
Page 13:	ACROSS: (3) into, (6) storm, (8) Jonah, (12) easy, (14) rope, (15) pray, (16) rescue, DOWN: (1) rough, (2) fish, (4) over, (5) Joppa, (7) map, (9) Nineveh, (10) help, (11) three, (13) sea, (17) up.
Page 14:	(c). After forty days Nineveh will be destroyed.
Page 15:	I the King declare that no-one is to eat or drink. Everyone must put on sackcloth and pray to God. We must stop doing anything which is bad. Perhaps God will stop being angry.
Page 17:	Jonah was very unhappy and became angry. He knew that God was loving and kind, and that he would change his mind. Jonah asked God to let him die.
Page 19:	Man's hair - bottom left, hat - top right, black stripe on jug, stripes on turban - bottom right, black sheep, pegs - top left, crook handle, patch on sack, peg on wheel, horn on oxen.
Page 23:	1 (c), 2 (b), 3 (c), 4 (a), 5 (c), 6 (c), 7 (a), 8 (b), 9 (c), 10 (a), 11 (b), 12 (b), 13 (b), 14 (a).

Text by Ruth Maclean,
Illustrations by Barrie Appleby
ISBN 978-1-85792-228-8

Reprinted 2009
Published by Christian Focus Publications, Geanies House, Fearn,
Ross-shire, IV20 1TW, Scotland, U.K.
Printed and bound by Bell and Bain, Glasgow

The text and answers are based on the New International Version of the Bible.